THE SIGNIFICANCE OF
RIBBON COLOURS
ON MEDALS WORN SINCE 1815 BY
AUSTRALIANS

Rick Grebert

Copyright © Rick Grebert, 2007

All rights reserved. No part of this publication may be reproduced or stored in a retrieval system by any means, electronic or mechanical, including photocopying, without prior permission in writing from the publisher.

Cataloguing-in-publication entry:
Grebert, Rick, 1947-
The Significance of **Ribbon Colours** on Medals worn since 1815 by Australians.

Bibliography
Includes Index
ISBN   1 876713 18 6

Published by Landers Publishing
PO Box 3082
Dural NSW 2158
AUSTRALIA

THE AUSTRALIAN ARMY HISTORY COLLECTION
This book is a joint venture with
The Australian Army History Unit

Front cover:
A selection of ribbons worn by Australians

Back cover:
Field Marshal Sir Thomas Blamey

**Dedicated to Australians
who wear Medal Ribbons**

*"What is a ribbon worth?
Everything!
Glory is priceless!"*

- Sir E.B. Lytton (1831-1891)

Foreword

As Head of the Defence Personnel Executive I am intimately involved in the matter of Honours and Awards within the Australian Defence Force. I am pleased, therefore, to have been given this chance to provide a short foreword to Rick Grebert's book on medal ribbons.

Many people often view the ribbon of a medal as simply a coloured strip of cloth with little or no significance in its own right. This is far from the case, especially for serving members of the defence forces who habitually wear ribbons as undress riband bars, without any medals, on their daily uniforms. To the knowledgeable, especially the knowledgeable amongst their uniformed compatriots, the colours of the ribbons immediately tell a story of service and, often, sacrifice.

Australians, including people who were born in the various colonies that would one day form the nation of Australia, have fought in Britain's, the Empire's and Australia's wars at least as far back as the Napoleonic Wars. It is known, for example, that British officers and soldiers who had been born in the infant colony of New South Wales were at the famous Battle of Waterloo in 1815. The ribbons of the various medals from that battle up until the deployments of the current day tell a stirring tale of service and sacrifice.

Rick Grebert has made a major contribution to the study of Australian military history and heraldry with his book on the significance of ribbon colours on medals worn by Australians since 1815. I believe that this book will become a standard reference work. I commend the hard work that has gone into the production of the book and wish Rick well for its success and in his future endeavours.

Major General Mark Evans, DSC, AM
Head, Defence Personnel Executive
August 2006

Contents

Foreword 4

Acknowledgements 6

Abbreviations 8

Introduction 10

British Orders, Decorations and Medals 13
awarded to Australians

The Australian Honours System 41

United Nations and NATO Medals 71
awarded to Australians

Foreign Orders, Decorations and Medals 87
awarded to Australians

Association and other Unofficial Medals 103
worn by Australians

Medal Ribbon Manufacturing Process 117

The Order of Wearing 121
Australian Honours and Awards

Bibliography 127

Index 130

Acknowledgements

Numerous organisations and individuals contributed to this publication in many different ways. I thank them all for their assistance and list them below in no particular order.

Ms Margaret Varghese, from the office of Awards and National Symbols Branch, Department of the Prime Minister and Cabinet, Canberra, who kindly provided detailed information about the Australian Honours System. The Directorate of Honours and Awards, Canberra, who provided much appreciated comment and advice. The Army History Unit, Department of Defence, Canberra, for supporting and coordinating this publication. Staff at RAAF HQ, Canberra. Mrs Karen Rigby, from KC Medals, Sydney, was most generous with her time and provided samples of the Australian Honours System ribbons, the United Nations medal ribbons and the original silk Allied Victory Medal ribbon.

Mr Robin Wright, Managing Director, The Wyedean Weaving Company Ltd, England, who kindly provided details about the medal ribbon manufacturing process.

Thanks also to Mr J.C. van Ingen, Director, Chancellery of Orders of Knighthood of the Kingdom of the Netherlands, The Hague. Susan Holgate, from the office of the Consulate General of the Kingdom of the Netherlands, Sydney. Peter Gilbert, from the office of the United States of America Consulate General, Sydney. G. Botsiou, from the office of the Consulate General of Greece, Sydney. Paul Bauwens, Consul, from the office of the Consulate General of Belgium, Sydney. Marc Finaud, from the office of the Consulat General de France, Sydney. Natalia Kanashchenko, Vice Consul, from the office of the Consulate General of the Russian Federation, Sydney. Tran Van Minh, Consul, from the office of the Consulate General of the Socialist Republic of Vietnam.

Mrs E.M. Bullock, from the Army Medal Office, Ministry of Defence, England. Dariusz Chmiel, Consul, from the office of the Consulate General of the Republic of Poland, Sydney. The office of the British High Commission, Canberra. Dr Wojciech Gorski OAM, from the Polish Ex-Servicemen's Association, Perth. Ms Jane Peek, from the Australian War Memorial, Canberra. Mr Mike Shepherd, from the Orders and Medals Research Society (Ribbon Branch), England. Mr Peter Porteous, from the Pacific Islands Regiment Association, Sydney. Mr Gordon Hughes, from the Rats of Tobruk Association, Sydney. Mr Des Pegram, from the BCOF Veterans Association, Sydney.

Mr Barry Brooks from the HMAS Sydney Association, Sydney. Ms Toni Smith from the office of the United Nations, Sydney. Mr Greg Read SC and Mr John Charter, from the ANZAC Memorial, Hyde Park, Sydney. Mr Bruce Beck and Mr Alf Carpenter, from the 2/4th Australian Infantry Battalion Association, Sydney. Mr Col Taylor, from the 2/9th Australian Infantry Battalion Association, Sydney. Mr Neil Russell, from the 2/12th Australian Infantry Battalion Association, Sydney. Mr Barry Presgrave OAM and Mr Ray Ayres, from the National Servicemen's Association of Australia, Adelaide. Mr Kim Clare, from RSM Awards International, Sydney. Mr Warwick Cary, Cary Corporation Pty Ltd, Sans Souci, Mr Greg Grebert, Glenbrook. Mr Rick Landers, Dural. The Australian War Memorial, Canberra and The State Library of NSW, Sydney.

Medal ribbon photography by the author.

Abbreviations

AATTV	Australian Army Training Team Vietnam
AC	Companion of the Order of Australia
AD	Dame of the Order of Australia
AFC	Air Force Cross
AFM	Air Force Medal
AIF	Australian Imperial Force
AK	Knight of the Order of Australia
AM	Member of the Order of Australia
ANZAC	Australian and New Zealand Army Corps
AO	Officer of the Order of Australia
BCOF	British Commonwealth Occupation Forces
BEM	British Empire Medal
c.	circa (about, approximate year)
Capt	Captain
CBE	Commander of the Order of the British Empire
DBE	Dame Commander of the Order of the British Empire
DFC	Distinguished Flying Cross
DFM	Distinguished Flying Medal
DSM	Distinguished Service Medal
Ed	Editor

GBE	Knight Grand Cross of the Order of the British Empire
HMAS	Her Majesty's Australian Ship
HQ	Headquarters
Inc	Incorporated
KBE	Knight Commander of the Order of the British Empire
Ltd	Limited
MBE	Member of the Order of the British Empire
NATO	North Atlantic Treaty Organisation
OAM	Medal of the Order of Australia
OBE	Officer of the Order of the British Empire
PIB	Papuan Infantry Battalion
PO	Post Office
RAAF	Royal Australian Air Force
RAN	Royal Australian Navy
RAR	Royal Australian Regiment
SC	Star of Courage
UN	United Nations
USA	United States of America
VC	Victoria Cross

Introduction

The medals and ribbon bars that are worn on the chest of a soldier summarise the service of that soldier. This publication explains the significance of the ribbon colours. Is the coloured cloth a ribbon or a riband?

Ribbon
n......c.1325 'Riban' – strip of cord or cloth; borrowed from Old French 'riban' a ribbon......The spelling 'rybban' appeared in 1446, and 'rybben' in 1545; ...... 'ribbon' was first used in Shakespeare's A Winter's Tale, in 1611.
(Chambers Dictionary of Etymology)

Riband
1870 Dickens...... The housemaids had been bribed with various fragments of 'riband'.
(The Oxford English Dictionary)

When a piece of ribbon is on a roll or loose it is 'ribbon'. When it becomes attached to a medal or is made into an undress bar, it becomes 'riband'.

In England in 1519, Knights were permitted to wear the 'Order of the Garter' (Lesser George) suspended by a chain, silk lace or black riband. In 1622, the riband colour was changed to light blue and King George II later changed the colour to dark blue.

The first medals for *military* service to be given in England were ordered to be struck by King Charles I. The Warrant was dated from the Court of Oxford on 18 May 1643. The medals were to be awarded to soldiers who distinguished themselves in *Forlorn Hopes.*

The first medal to be issued to all officers and enlisted men was awarded by the Island of St Vincent, West Indies, in 1773. The medal was given to the entire Militia for suppressing an insurrection by the Carib Indians. **This was the first general issue medal to be suspended from a riband.**

Ribands replaced chains in 1794, when the first 'Regulation Riband' was instituted. The '***Naval*** *Riband of England*' was white with a broad navy blue stripe on both edges. This riband was used on the 'Naval General Service Medal' (1793-1840). The '***Military*** *Riband of England*' was crimson with a dark blue stripe on both edges. This riband was used on the:

> Military General Service Medal (1793-1814);
> Army Gold Medals and Peninsula Gold Cross (1806-1814);
> Waterloo Medal (1815);
> First Burma War Medal (1824-1826);
> Distinguished Service Order (established 1886).

With the ever-increasing number of military medals being introduced, it was decided in 1839 that other riband colours would be introduced, instead of using the regulation colours of the '*Military Riband of England*'. This eventually led to the introduction of multi-coloured ribands, which helped to differentiate one medal from another.

At some stage after the instigation of medal wearing, when not on ceremonial duty, slots were cut in the tunic of the wearer through which to thread the medal out of sight, so that it did not become damaged. This left only the riband on show and led to the adoption of riband bars for ceremonial dress wear, for other than on full dress occasions.

Queen Victoria 'invented' miniature medals. She became annoyed at the continual clanking of medals worn by old soldiers in her presence. She declared that half size versions should be used for evening wear, mess-dress etc.

Widespread use of ribands on medals seems to have begun early in the nineteenth century. Early in the twenty-first century, the names riband and ribbon were both used in publications, although ribbon was more commonly used.

Rick Grebert, FNSWMHS
Sydney, NSW
AUSTRALIA

British Orders, Decorations and Medals Awarded to Australians

Since 1992, British (Imperial) awards to Australians have been regarded as 'foreign' awards.

Many of the British Orders, Decorations and Medals that were awarded to Australians are not included in this publication, because their **ribbon colours have no known significance**. This situation was confirmed by the Ministry of Defence (Army Medal Office) in England and the Orders and Medals Research Society (Ribbon Branch) in England.

Union Flag

Victoria Cross
Established in 1856
[Great Britain]

Army VC

Navy VC

Ribbon colours

When the Victoria Cross was established in 1856, the ribbon colour was the crimson of the Military Riband of England for the Army and the navy blue of the Naval Riband of England for the Navy. (See Introduction). Following the formation of the Royal Air Force in 1918, it was decided by Royal Warrant in 1920 that crimson ribbon would be used for all three Services.

The crimson symbolises blood and love.
The blue symbolises the sky and Royal Majesty.

Captain Neville Reginald Howse. NSW Army Medical Corps (Boer War). Australia's first Victoria Cross recipient (1900). Victoria Cross, South Africa 1899-1902 (Queen's Medal), 1914-15 Star, British War Medal, Allied Victory Medal.

Supplement in *Illustrated London News* 20 June 1857 six days before first investiture in London by Queen Victoria

Supplement in *Illustrated London News* 20 June 1857 six days before first investiture in London by Queen Victoria

George Cross
Established in 1940
[Great Britain]

Ribbon colour

The kingfisher blue ribbon colour on the George Cross is in keeping with the ribbon colour change, to kingfisher blue, for the Order of the Garter. The colour change was made during the reign of King George VI and the George Cross was established during His reign.

The original George Cross Warrant dated 24 September 1940 was cancelled by a new Warrant dated 8 May 1941.

Order of the Garter
Established in 1348
[England]

Ribbon colour

The earliest Garters were black and were worn below the knee to indicate the dignity of the Order. With the introduction of coloured medal ribands (1622), the sash of the Order of the Garter was originally made light blue (blue was the colour of Royal Majesty). With dynasty changes over the years, the blue was changed to darker shades of blue, to differentiate the different dynasties. During the reign of King George VI, kingfisher blue was introduced.

This Order belongs not to the United Kingdom, but to **England** alone.

The Order of the Garter was bestowed on three Australians. They were Governors-General:

Baron Casey (1969);
Sir Paul Hasluck (1979);
Sir Ninian Stephen (1994).

Order of the Thistle

Established in 1540
Revived in 1687
[Great Britain]

Ribbon colour

Dark green is the colour of the thistle plant.

The only Australian born person to be created a Knight of the Order of the Thistle was Sir Robert Menzies (1963).

Order of the Bath

Established in 1399
Revived in 1725
[Great Britain]

Ribbon colour

The Order consists of the Sovereign, a Prince of the **blood** Royal.... Red was often used to symbolise blood and love.

The ribbon colour is blood red.

Order of Merit

Established in 1902
[Great Britain]

Ribbon colours

Blue represents the ribbon of the Order of the Garter. Crimson represents the ribbon of the Order of the Bath.

Order of St Michael and St George

Established in 1818
[Great Britain]

Ribbon colours

These ribbon colours carry on the tradition of the *Military Riband of England*. (See Introduction). It consists of a crimson centre stripe, with navy blue edge stripes. The crimson symbolises blood and love. The blue symbolises the sky and Royal Majesty.

Order of the British Empire

Established in 1917
[Great Britaian]

First Ribbon (1917-1937)

General Division — Military Division

Second Ribbon (since 1937)

General Division — Military Division

Ribbon colours

When the Order was established in June 1917, the ribbon colours were purple (the colour of Kings), with a narrow scarlet stripe down the centre for the Military Division of the Order (established in December 1918).

In 1937, following the death of King George V, Queen Mary had the ribbon colours changed to rose pink, with narrow pearl-grey stripes down the edges. A central stripe, also of pearl-grey, was added for the Military Division of the Order.

The second type ribbon may be worn instead of the first type, but not vice versa.

The six classes of the Order:
- Knight/Dame Grand Cross of the Order of the British Empire (GBE).
- Knight/Dame Commander of the Order of the British Empire (KBE/DBE).
- Commander of the Order of the British Empire (CBE).
- Officer of the Order of the British Empire (OBE).
- Member of the Order of the British Empire (MBE).
- British Empire Medal (BEM).

Distinguished Service Order

Established in 1886
[Great Britain]

Ribbon colours

These ribbon colours carry on the tradition of the *Military Riband of England*. (See Introduction). The crimson symbolises blood and love. The blue symbolises the sky and Royal Majesty.

Distinguished Conduct Medal

Established in 1845
[Great Britain]

Ribbon colours

These ribbon colours carry on the tradition of the *Military Riband of England*. (See Introduction). The crimson symbolises blood and love. The blue symbolises the sky and Royal Majesty.

Sergeant Alexander Davidson Sutherland. 7th Battalion, The Royal Australian Regiment. Distinguished Conduct Medal (awarded during the Vietnam War), Australian Active Service Medal (Vietnam), Korea Medal, United Nations Service Medal Korea, Vietnam Medal, Australian Service Medal (Malaya), Defence Force Service Medal, National Medal, Republic of Vietnam Campaign Medal (Star).

Waterloo Medal
(1815)
[Great Britain]

Ribbon colours

These ribbon colours carry on the tradition of the Military Riband of England. (See Introduction). The crimson symbolises blood and love. The blue symbolises the sky and Royal Majesty.

Australian at Waterloo.

Lieutenant Douglas White was the son of the Surgeon General on the First Fleet. He was born in Sydney, Australia, in 1793, and served at Waterloo.

New Zealand Medal 1845-1866

(Maori Wars)
[Great Britain]

Ribbon colours

These ribbon colours carry on the tradition of the Military Riband of England. (See Introduction). The crimson symbolises blood and love. The blue symbolises the sky and Royal Majesty.

Australians at the New Zealand War.

Australian Soldiers of Fortune were recruited for service in New Zealand in 1863-1864. They formed part of the Waikato Regiments. The Australian Colonies did not send contingents to this war.

2,410 medals were issued to Australians.

Egypt Medal 1882-1889

(Soudan War)
[Great Britain]

Ribbon colours

Blue stripes represent the *Blue Nile River.*
White stripes represent the *White Nile River.*

The NSW Soudan Contingent, 1885, was the first Expeditionary Force from Australia. Recipients of the *Egypt Medal* also received the *Khedive's Star 1884-1886*. There were 771 men in the Contingent.

Khedive's Star 1884-1886
[Ribbon colour has no known significance]

Australia's first Battle Honour

Third China War Medal 1900

(Boxer Rebellion)
[Great Britain]

Ribbon colours

Crimson is the Heraldic colour of Great Britain.
Yellow is the Imperial colour of China.

554 medals were issued to the Australian Colonies (NSW, Victoria and South Australia).

South Africa 1899-1902

Queen's Medal (Anglo-Boer War)
[Great Britain]

Ribbon colours

Crimson represents the Army.
Navy blue represents the Navy.
Orange represents the veldt in South Africa.

15,160 medals were issued to Australians.

South Africa 1901-1902
King's Medal (Anglo-Boer War)
[Great Britain]

Ribbon colours

Green appears in the flag of the Transvaal Republic.
Orange appears in the flag of the Orange Free State.
White is common to both flags.

744 medals were issued to Australians.

Natal Rebellion Medal 1906
(Zulu Rising)
[Great Britain]

Ribbon colours

Crimson represents the British Colonial Forces (Imperial troops did not serve).
Black represents the Zulus.

Australians at the Natal Rebellion

Australia did not send troops to the Natal Rebellion. However, a few Australians served in various colonial units. Their medals are named to the colonial units in which they served.

1914 Star ('Mons' Star)
and
1914-15 Star
[Great Britain]

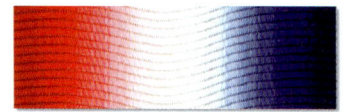

Ribbon colours

Red, white and blue are the colours of the United Kingdom and the Union Flag ('Union Jack') of the United Kingdom. The ribbon is shaded and watered.

Approximately 123 1914 Stars and 82,000 1914-15 Stars were issued to Australians.

Union Flag

Mercantile Marine War Medal 1914-1918

[Great Britain]

Ribbon colours

Colours of a ship's navigation lights:
Green – the starboard side light.
White – the steaming light.
Red – the port side light.

Approximately 12,000 medals were issued to Australians.

Allied Victory Medal 1914-1918

[Great Britain]

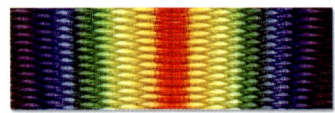

Ribbon colours

The colours of the rainbow are duplicated, shaded and watered, to represent a double rainbow.

In 1919, the Allied and associated powers held a conference in Paris to decide on a common War Medal. It was decided that the name of the medal should be such that the Germans could not use the same name. The chosen name was the Victory Medal. It was also decided that each country would produce their own medal, but use the same ribbon. To satisfy the numerous ideas put forward, a rainbow coloured ribbon was the most popular choice. However, Britain objected because the ribbon for the 1914 Star and 1914-15 Star was similar to a rainbow, so the final decision was to use a double rainbow ribbon for the Victory Medal.

Approximately 336,000 medals were issued to Australians.

1939-45 Star

[Great Britain]

Ribbon colours

Navy blue represents the Naval Forces and Merchant Navies.
Red represents the Armies.
Light blue represents the Air Forces.

202,694 stars were issued to Australians.

Atlantic Star

[Great Britain]

Ribbon colours

Blue, white and sea green are symbolical of the waters of the Atlantic Ocean. The ribbon is shaded and watered.

6,046 stars were issued to Australians

Air Crew Europe Star
[Great Britain]

Ribbon colours

Black and yellow represent continuous service by day and night. Light blue represents the Air Forces.

3,165 stars were issued to Australians.

Africa Star
[Great Britain]

Ribbon colours

Beige represents the sands of the Western Desert.
Navy blue represents the Naval Forces and Merchant Navies.
Red represents the Armies.
Light blue represents the Air Forces.

42,457 stars were issued to Australians.

Pacific Star
[Great Britain]

Ribbon colours

Red represents the Armies.
Navy blue represents the Naval Forces and the Merchant Navies.
Green and yellow represent the jungles and beaches of the Pacific region.
Light blue represents the Air Forces.

204,706 stars were issued to Australians.

Burma Star
[Great Britain]

Ribbon colours

Orange represents the sun.
Red represents the British Commonwealth Forces.

5,047 stars were issued to Australians.

Italy Star
[Great Britain]

Ribbon colours

Red, white and green are the colours of the Italian flag.

4,640 stars were issued to Australians.

Italian Flag

France and Germany Star
[Great Britain]

Ribbon colours

Blue, white and red are the colours of the United Kingdom and the Union flag ('Union Jack') of the United Kingdom and the colours of the flags of France and the Netherlands.

4,687 stars were issued to Australians.

Union Flag

French Flag

Netherlands Flag

Defence Medal 1939-45

[Great Britain]

Ribbon colours

Flame colour in the centre of green, representing the enemy attacks on our green land. The black represents the blackouts.

82,392 medals were issued to Australians.

War Medal 1939-45

[Great Britain]

Ribbon colours

Red, white and blue are the colours of the United Kingdom and the Union flag ('Union Jack') of the United Kingdom.

247,434 medals were issued to Australians.

Union Flag

Australian Service Medal 1939-45

[Great Britain/Australia]

Ribbon colours

Navy blue represents the RAN.
Red represents the Mercantile Marine.
Khaki Represents the Australian Army.
Light blue represents the RAAF.

177,290 medals were issued to Australians.

Although this is an Australian Service Medal, it is part of the Imperial Awards System.

Korea Medal
[Great Britain]

Ribbon colours

Blue is the colour of the United Nations flag.
Yellow is the traditional colour used by the British for service in the Orient.

Approximately 16,000 medals were issued to Australians.

Recipients of this medal also received the *United Nations Service Medal, Korea 1950-54*. The UN medal was authorised to be worn by Australian recipients as a campaign medal next to the Korea Medal. All other *UN* medals are worn at the end of medal groups. See the '*United Nations and NATO Medals Awarded to Australians*' section of this book.

Approximately 18,000 *United Nations Service Medals* were issued to Australians (some did not qualify for the *Korea Medal*).

United Nations Flag

Vietnam Medal

Established in 1968
[Great Britain/Australia]

Ribbon colours

Navy blue represents the RAN.
Light blue represents the RAAF.
The two thick red stripes represent the Australian Army.
The yellow and three central red stripes represent the flag of the Republic of Vietnam.

Only Australian and New Zealand troops were awarded the *Vietnam Medal*.

49,708 Vietnam Medals were issued to Australians.

The Republic of Vietnam Campaign Medal (Star) was also awarded for a minimum of six months service.

Although this is an Australian Service Medal, it is part of the Imperial Awards System.

Repubic of Vietnam Flag

Republic of Vietnam Campaign Medal (Star) (Ribbon colours have no known significance)

The Australian Honours System

Established in 1975

Australian Flag

Victoria Cross for Australia
Established in 1991
[Australia]

Ribbon colours

When the **Imperial Victoria Cross** was established in 1856, the ribbon colour of the Army VC was the crimson of the *Military Riband of England* and the ribbon colour of the Navy VC was the navy blue of the *Naval Riband of England*. (See Introduction). Following the formation of the Royal Air Force in 1918, it was determined by Royal Warrant of 1920 that crimson ribbon would be used for all three Services.

The crimson symbolises blood and love.
The blue symbolises the sky and Royal Majesty.

The **Victoria Cross for Australia** was established as part of the Australian system of Honours and Awards, on 15 January 1991. It continued the proud tradition of Australian access to this award since its institution by Queen Victoria in 1856. There were 96 Australian recipients of the 'Imperial VC' between 1900 and 1969. The 'VC for Australia' has yet to be awarded (2007). **The 'Imperial VC' and 'VC for Australia' differ in name only.**

Cross of Valour
Established in 1975
[Australia]

Ribbon colours

The central bright red stripe represents arterial blood (oxygenated) and the dark red (magenta) edge stripes represent venous blood (de-oxygenated).

There have been five awards of the Cross of Valour (2007):
Darrell James TREE   1989;
Victor Alan BOSCOE   1995;
Allan John SPARKES   1998;
Timothy Ian BRITTEN   2003;
Richard John JOYES   2003.

Order of Australia

Established in 1975
[Australia]

General Division

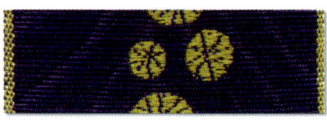
Military Division

Ribbon colours

The gold discs represent Golden Wattle flowers.
Gold edge stripes are added for the Military Division.

Gold and royal blue are the livery (Heraldic) colours on the Commonwealth of Australia Coat of Arms. The Coat of Arms was assigned to the Commonwealth of Australia by Royal Warrant on 19 September 1912.

The five classes of the Order:
- Knight/Dame of the Order of Australia   AK/AD*
- Companion of the Order of Australia   AC
- Officer of the Order of Australia   AO
- Member of the Order of Australia   AM
- Medal of the Order of Australia (from 1976)   OAM

*   Provision for the appointment of Knights and Dames of the Order of Australia was introduced in 1976 by Prime Minister Malcolm Fraser and removed in 1986 by Prime Minister Bob Hawke. (Eleven Knights and two Dames were created).

Australia's Floral Emblem is Acacia Pycnantha (Golden Wattle). In Australia, Acacia has always been known as Wattle. In Europe and the USA, Acacia is known as Mimosa.

Golden Wattle

Commonwealth of Australia
Coat of Arms

Star of Gallantry

Established in 1991
[Australia]

Ribbon colours

Light and dark orange symbolise the heat of action – continuing the theme of stylised flames on the Star. There are also stylised 'A's for Australia on the ribbon.

Star of Courage

Established in 1975
[Australia]

Ribbon colours

The central dark red (magenta) stripe represents venous blood (de-oxygenated) and the bright red edge stripes represent arterial blood (oxygenated).

Distinguished Service Cross

Established in 1991
[Australia]

Ribbon colours

Ochre red represents service in warlike operations, for which the cross is awarded.

Conspicuous Service Cross

Established in 1989
[Australia]

Ribbon colours

Sandy yellow stripes represent the Golden Wattle flower and the Australian sand. Green stripes represent the Australian bush.

Nursing Service Cross

Established in 1989
[Australia]

Ribbon colours

Red and white are the colours of the Red Cross. Yellow edge stripes represent the military nature of the award.

Red Cross Flag

Medal for Gallantry

Established in 1991
[Australia]

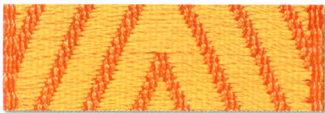

Ribbon colours

Light and dark orange symbolise the heat of action – continuing the theme of stylised flames on the Medal. There are also stylised 'A's for Australia on the ribbon.

Bravery Medal

Established in 1975
[Australia]

Ribbon colours

Alternating bright red and dark red stripes represent arterial (oxygenated) and venous (de-oxygenated) blood respectively.

Distinguished Service Medal

Established in 1991
[Australia]

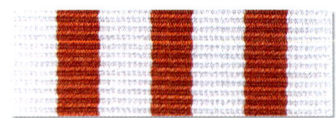

Ribbon colours

Ochre red stripes represent service in warlike operations, for which the Medal is awarded.

Public Service Medal

Established in 1989
[Australia]

Ribbon colours

Green and gold are Australia's national colours.

Australian Police Medal

Established in 1986
[Australia]

Ribbon colours

Navy blue and white are the colours of the Australian Police Services.

Australian Fire Service Medal

Established in 1988
[Australia]

Ribbon colours

Green and gold are Australia's national colours. The red symbolic flames represent the challenge of the fire service.

Ambulance Service Medal

Established in 1999
[Australia]

Ribbon colours

Red and white are the traditional ambulance colours. Silver represents excellence.

Emergency Services Medal
Established in 1999
[Australia]

Ribbon colours

The orange and white chequerboard pattern is used by all emergency services in Australia. The blue edge stripes represent marine rescue.

Conspicuous Service Medal
Established in 1989
[Australia]

Ribbon colours

Sandy yellow stripes represent the Golden Wattle flower and the Australian sand. Green stripes represent the Australian bush.

Australian Antarctic Medal

Established in 1987
[Australia]

Ribbon colours

Snow-white moire with edge stripes consisting of three shades of blue merging into the white represent the ice of the Antarctic and the surrounding sea.

Commendation for Gallantry

Established in 1991
[Australia]

Ribbon colour

Dark orange symbolises the heat of action.

Commendation for Brave Conduct

Established in 1975
[Australia]

Ribbon colour

Bright red represents arterial (oxygenated) blood.

Commendation for Distinguished Service

Established in 1991
[Australia]

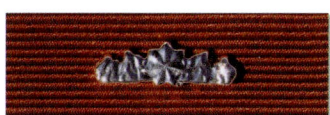

Ribbon colour

Ochre red represents service in warlike operations, for which the Commendation is awarded.

Australian Active Service Medal
(1945-1975)

Established in 1997
[Australia]

Ribbon colours

Purple, green, blue, yellow and red are colours used on Imperial medal ribbons issued for campaign service between 1945 and 1975.

Vietnam Logistic and Support Medal

Established in 1993
[Australia]

Ribbon colours

Navy blue represents the RAN.
Light blue represents the RAAF.
The thick red stripe represents the Australian Army.
Brown represents the earth and the colour of the inland and coastal waterways of Vietnam.
The yellow and three central red stripes represent the flag of the Republic of Vietnam.

Repubic of Vietnam Flag

Australian Active Service Medal
(since 1975)

Established in 1991
[Australia]

Ribbon colours

Primarily variations of the Australian colours – green and gold. The red stripe represents the dangers faced in warlike situations on active service.

International Force East Timor Medal (INTERFET)

Established in 2000
[Australia]

Ribbon colours

Green represents the Army and re-growth of a new nation.
Red represents the turbulent past of East Timor.
White represents the Navy and peace.
Blue represents the Air Force and the sea.

Afghanistan Campaign Medal

Established in 2004
[Australia]

Ribbon colours

Light blue represents the sky above the mountains in Afghanistan.
White represents the snow on the mountain peaks.
Khaki represents the dominant ground colour of the terrain.
Purple represents the three arms of the Australian Defence Force. Purple is the combination of navy blue, red and light blue – the colours that represent the RAN, Army and RAAF respectively.
Red represents the conflict in Afghanistan

Iraq Campaign Medal

Established in 2004
[Australia]

Ribbon colours

Sand yellow represents the desert sands of Iraq.
Purple represents the three arms of the Australian Defence Force. Purple is the combination of navy blue, red and light blue – the colours that represent the RAN, Army and RAAF respectively.
Red represents the conflict in Iraq.

Australian Service Medal
(1945-1975)

Established in 1995
[Australia]

Ribbon colours

Light and navy blue and khaki represent the Australian Armed Forces. Green and gold are Australia's national colours.

Australian Service Medal
(since 1975)

Established in 1988
[Australia]

Ribbon colours

The colours represent the Australian bush and earth.

Rhodesia Medal
Established in 1980
[Australia]

Ribbon colours

Blue-grey is a neutral colour that is not represented on the flag of any of the Commonwealth Monitoring Force countries and is not the UN blue.

Red, white and blue are the colours of the Union flag *('Union Jack')* of the United Kingdom.

152 medals were issued to Australians.

Recipients of this 'Australian Medal' also received the *Zimbabwe Independence Medal (Commonwealth Monitoring Force -* Australia, New Zealand, Fiji and Kenya).

Union Flag

Police Overseas Service Medal

Established in 1991
[Australia]

Ribbon colours

Chequerboard pattern of the police service in black and white.

Humanitarian Overseas Service Medal

Established in 1999
[Australia]

Ribbon colours

Eucalyptus green represents regeneration.
Gold represents the Australian sun, optimism and hope.

Civilian Service Medal 1939-1945

Established in 1994
[Australia]

Ribbon colours

Green represents the land and food production.
Ochre represents the soil of Australia.
White stripes represent communications and construction.

80th Anniversary Armistice Remembrance Medal

Established in 1998
[Australia]

Ribbon colours

Red and black represent the red petals and black centre of the Flanders poppy, which is associated with the Western Front during World War I. This poppy has been a symbol of remembrance ever since.

The medal was awarded to Australian veterans of World War I who survived to the 80th anniversary of the Armistice - 11th November 1998. Sixty-six veterans were living at the time of the 80th anniversary.

Flanders Poppy

Australian Sports Medal

Awarded only in 2000
(Sydney Olympics)
[Australia]

Ribbon colours

Green and gold are Australia's national colours and traditional sporting colours.

Centenary Medal

Established in 2001
[Australia]

Ribbon colours

Royal blue and gold are the *livery* colours on the Commonwealth of Australia Coat of Arms. Crimson represents Federation "*...the crimson thread of kinship*." (Sir Henry Parkes). The seven gold and crimson stripes represent the pathways to federation of the states – six stripes represent the six states and the seventh stripe represents Australia's territories.

Defence Force Service Medal

Established in 1982
[Australia]

Ribbon colours

Royal blue and gold are the *livery* colours on the Commonwealth of Australia Coat of Arms.

Reserve Force Decoration

Established in 1982
[Australia]

Ribbon colours

Royal blue and gold are the *livery* colours on the Commonwealth of Australia Coat of Arms.

Reserve Force Medal

Established in 1982
[Australia]

Ribbon colours

Royal blue and gold are the *livery* colours on the Commonwealth of Australia Coat of Arms.

Defence Long Service Medal

Established in 1998
[Australia]

Ribbon colours

Royal blue and gold are the *livery* colours on the Commonwealth of Australia Coat of Arms.

National Medal
Established in 1975
[Australia]

Ribbon colours

Royal blue and gold are the livery colours on the Commonwealth of Australia Coat of Arms. The fifteen stripes represent fifteen years of service.

Australian Defence Medal
Established in 2006
[Australia]

Ribbon colours

Black and red are the colours of the Flanders poppy, which represents the ANZAC spirit of the Australian Armed Forces. The white stripes represent peacetime service and the stripes also divide the red into three, representing the three Services.

Flanders Poppy

Australian Cadet Forces Service Medal

Established in 1999
[Australia]

Ribbon colours

Royal blue and gold are the *livery* colours on the Commonwealth of Australia Coat of Arms. The edge stripes of navy blue, red and light blue represent the Australian Cadet Force's links with the RAN, Australian Army and RAAF respectively.

Champion Shots Medal

Established in 1988
[Australia]

Ribbon colours

Light blue, red and navy blue represent the RAAF, Australian Army and RAN respectively.

Anniversary of National Service 1951-1972 Medal

Established in 2001
[Australia]

Ribbon colours

Ochre red represents the soils of Australia.
Light blue represents the RAAF.
Green represents the Australian Army.
White represents the RAN.
Royal blue and gold are the livery colours on the Commonwealth of Australia Coat of Arms.

Commonwealth of Australia
Coat of Arms

Unit Citations

Established in 1991
[Australia]

Unit Citation for Gallantry.

Meritorious Unit Citation.

Ribbon colours

Green and gold are Australia's national colours.

The insignia is a sterling silver frame, which has a pattern of flames indicating that the award was earned under active service conditions. The frame of the *Unit Citation for Gallantry* is gold plated and the frame of the *Meritorious Unit Citation* is rhodium plated. The Commonwealth Star on the ribbon indicates that the person wearing the insignia was a member of the unit when the Citation was awarded. Only members who were part of the Unit when the Citation was awarded are permitted to wear the insignia after they cease to be members of that unit.

The first Unit to be awarded the **Unit Citation for Gallantry** was Number 1 Squadron, Special Air Service Regiment, for service in Iraq in 2003.

United Nations and NATO Medals Awarded to Australians

United Nations and
NATO Flags

United Nations Headquarters (UNHQ)

Ribbon colour

United Nations blue.

United Nations Truce Supervision Organisation (UNTSO)

Established in 1948

Ribbon colours

Blue and white of the United Nations flag.

United Nations Military Observer Force in India and Pakistan (UNMOGIP)

Established in 1949

Ribbon colours

Various shades of green in the centre represent the Himalayan Range and the Kashmir Valley.
White stripes represent the snow-capped mountains.
Edge stripes of United Nations blue.

United Nations Service Medal Korea (UNSM)

1950-1954

Ribbon colours

Blue and white of the United Nations flag.
The 17 stripes represent the 17 combatant UN countries that served in Korea.

United Nations Operations in the Congo (ONUC)
1960-1964

Before 1963

Since 1963

Ribbon colours

Originally the ribbon was UN blue and white.
In 1963 a distinctive ribbon was issued. Green represented the Congo Basin and hope for the young nation.
Blue and white of the United Nations flag.

United Nations Yemen Observer Mission (UNYOM)
1963-1964

Ribbon colours

Various shades of brown represent the dry and rugged mountainous mass in Yemen.
Yellow represents the desert.
Edge stripes of United Nations blue.

United Nations Peacekeeping Force in Cyprus (UNFICYP)

Established in 1964

Ribbon colours

Blue and white of the United Nations flag.
Thin dark blue stripes represent the Mediterranean Sea.

United Nations Emergency Force II (UNEFII)

1973-1979

Ribbon colours

United Nations blue.
Yellow represents the sands of the Sinai Desert.
Thin dark blue stripes represent the Suez Canal.

United Nations Disengagement Observer Force – Golan Heights (UNDOF)

Established in 1974

Ribbon colours

The central red stripe flanked by blue stripes represent the United Nations Force within the De-Militarised Zone.
The black stripes represent the volcanic rocks of the Golan.
The white stripes represent the snow capped Mount Hermon Range.
The burgundy edge stripes represent the native thistles of the Golan Heights and the purple haze at sunset.

United Nations Iran/Iraq Military Observers Group (UNIIMOG)

1988-1991

Ribbon colours

United Nations blue.
Green, white and red stripes on the left represent the flag of Iran.
Red, white and black stripes on the right represent the flag of Iraq.

Iranian Flag

Iraqi Flag

United Nations Transition Assistance Group (UNTAG)

1989-1990

Ribbon colours

United Nations blue.
Yellow represents the sands of the Kalahari and Namib deserts.
Black, yellow, red, green and blue are the colours of the Olympic Rings which represent the five continental regions of the World, all of which were represented in UNTAG.

Olympic Rings

United Nations Mission for the Referendum in Western Sahara (MINURSO)

Established in 1991

Ribbon colours

Sandy brown represents the Sahara Desert.
United Nations blue.

The acronym is derived from the French – *Mission des nations unies pour le referendum dans le Sahara Occidental.*

United Nations Special Service Medal (UNSSM)

Established in 1992

Ribbon colours

Blue and white of the United Nations Flag.

United Nations Advance Mission in Cambodia (UNAMIC)

1991-1992

Ribbon colours

Red, gold, dark blue and white are the colours of the Cambodian flag. The light blue is United Nations blue.

Cambodian Flag

United Nations Protection Force (UNPROFOR)

1992-1995

Ribbon colours

Four stripes of United Nations blue.
Red represents the United Nations protected areas.
Green represents the forests.
Brown represents the mountains.

United Nations Transitional Authority in Cambodia (UNTAC)

1992-1993

Ribbon colours

Green represents the paddy fields which cover most of Cambodia. The red and white are the colours of all the factions' flags. United Nations blue and Supreme National Council dark blue.

United Nations Operations in Somalia (UNOSOM)

1992-1995

Ribbon colours

Yellow represents the desert.
Green represents hope.
United Nations blue.

United Nations Operations in Mozambique (ONUMOZ)

1992-1995

Ribbon colours

Green represents the tropical climate of Mozambique.
White represents peace.
United Nations blue.

United Nations Verification Mission in Guatemala (MINUGUA)

Established in 1994

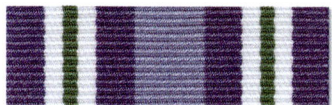

Ribbon colours

Central stripe of United Nations blue.
Blue, white and green are the colours of the Guatemala flag.

Guatemala Flag

United Nations Assistance for Rwanda (UNAMIR)

1993-1996

Ribbon colours

Blue and white of the United Nations flag.
Black represents the volcanic lava and the world famous gorillas of the area.
Green represents the local bush vegetation.
Red represents the African soil.

United Nations Assistance Mission in East Timor (UNAMET)

United Nations Transitional Administration in East Timor (UNTAET)

Established in 1999

Ribbon colours

Two outer stripes of UN blue.
Red and yellow represent the brilliant and spectacular sunrises and sunsets in East Timor.
White represents peace and hope.

NATO Kosovo Medal
Established in October 1998

Ribbon colours

Dark blue and white are the colours of the NATO flag.

NATO Former Yugoslavia Medal
Established in June 1992

Ribbon colours

Dark blue and white are the colours of the NATO flag.

NATO Flag

Foreign Orders, Decorations and Medals awarded to Australians

Many of the Foreign Orders, Decorations and Medals that were awarded to Australians are not included in this publication, because their **ribbon colours have no known significance.**

Foreign awards were presented to Australians by: Belgium, Denmark, Egypt, France, Greece, Hejaz, Italy, Kuwait, Lebanon, Montenegro, Netherlands, Papua New Guinea, Poland, Portugal, Republic of Vietnam, Romania, Russia, Saudi Arabia, Serbia, the United States of America and Zimbabwe.

Liberation of Kuwait Medal
1991
[Kuwait]

Ribbon colours

Red, white and green are the colours of the National Flag of Kuwait.

Kuwaiti Flag.

Order of Orange Nassau
(Orde Van Oranje Nassau)
Established in 1892
[Netherlands]

Ribbon colours

Orange is the national colour of the Netherlands.
Orange and Nassau blue represent the Dutch Royal House.
The significance of the white is not known.

This order was awarded to 12 Australians in World War Two.

Bronze Cross
(Bronzen Kruis)
Established in 1940
[Netherlands]

Ribbon colours

Orange is the national colour of the Netherlands.
Orange and Nassau blue represent the Dutch Royal House.

This cross was awarded to six Australians in World War Two.

Cross of Merit
(Kruis Voor Verdienste)
Established in 1941
[Netherlands]

Ribbon colours

Orange is the national colour of the Netherlands.
Orange and Nassau blue represent the Dutch Royal House.

This cross was awarded to one Australian in World War Two.

Flying Cross
(Vliegerkruis)
Established in 1941
[Netherlands]

British DFC

Ribbon colours

Orange is the national colour of the Netherlands.
The diagonal stripes design on the ribbon is that of the British *Distinguished Flying Cross.*

This cross was awarded to four Australians in World War Two.

Medal for Acts of Humanity
(Erepenning Voor Menslievend Hulpbetoon)
Established in 1822
[Netherlands]

Ribbon colours

Orange is the national colour of the Netherlands.
Red represents sacrifice.

This medal was awarded to three Australian civilians in 1945 for saving life following the crash of a Dutch military aircraft in Australia.

Papua New Guinea Independence Medal 1975

[Papua New Guinea]

Ribbon colours

Red, black, white and gold are the colours of the National Flag of Papua New Guinea.

Papua New Guinea 10th Anniversary of Independence Medal 1985

[Papua New Guinea]

Ribbon colours

Red, black, white and gold are the colours of the National Flag of Papua New Guinea.

Papua New Guinea Flag

Cross of Valour
(Krzyz Walecznych)

Established in 1920
[Poland]

Ribbon colours

Red and white are the Polish national colours and national flag colours.

This cross was awarded to a few Australian Rats of Tobruk and also to a few RAAF personnel in the European Theatre of War, in World War Two.

Order of Military Virtue
(Virtuti Militari)

Established in 1792
Revived in 1919
[Poland]

Ribbon colours

Azure (sky) blue and black are the colours of the uniforms that were worn by Polish regiments in 1792, when this Order was established.

This order was awarded to two Australians in World War Two.

Liberation of Kuwait Medal

1990-1992
[Saudi Arabia]

Ribbon colours

Green and white are the colours of the National Flag of Saudi Arabia.

Saudi Arabian Flag

Distinguished Service Cross (Army)

Established in 1918
[United States of America]

Ribbon colours

Red represents sacrifice. White represents purity. Blue represents high purpose. Red, white and blue are also the National colours and the colours of the National Flag of the USA.

This cross was awarded to five Australians in World War One, 17 in World War Two and one in the Vietnam War.

Distinguished Service Medal (Army)

Established in 1918
[United States of America]

Ribbon colours

The DSM is given for "…..service less conspicuous than that for which the Medal of Honor is given". So, it was decided that the ribbon should be red, in keeping with the tradition that red ribbon is usually associated with the second prize. Red, white and blue are also the National colours and the colours of the National Flag of the USA.

This medal was awarded to 12 Australians in World War One.

Silver Star
Established in 1932
[United States of America]

Ribbon colours

Red, white and blue are the national colours and the colours of the National Flag of the USA. Red symbolises courage, zeal and fervency. White symbolises purity and rectitude of conduct. Blue symbolises loyalty, devotion, friendship, justice and truth.

This star was awarded to 28 Australians in World War Two and 30 in the Vietnam War.

Distinguished Flying Cross
Established in 1926
Retroactive to 1917-1918
[United States of America]

Ribbon colours

Red, white and blue are the National colours and the colours of the National Flag of the USA. Red symbolises courage, zeal and fervency. White symbolises purity and rectitude of conduct. Blue symbolises loyalty, devotion, friendship, justice and truth.

This cross was awarded to 27 Australians in World War Two.

Soldiers Medal

Established in 1926
[United States of America]

Ribbon colours

Red, white and blue are the national colours and the colours of the National Flag of the USA.

Red symbolises courage, zeal and fervency. White symbolises purity and rectitude of conduct. Blue symbolises loyalty, devotion, friendship, justice and truth.

The 13 red and white stripes represent the 13 stripes on the Shield of the US Coat of Arms, which symbolise the first 13 United States.

This medal was awarded to 11 Australians in World War Two and three in the Vietnam War.

USA Flag

Shield of the USA
Coat of Arms.

Bronze Star

Established in 1944
[United States of America]

Ribbon colours

Red, white and blue are the National colours and the colours of the National Flag of the USA.
Red symbolises courage, zeal and fervency.
White symbolises purity and rectitude of conduct.
Blue symbolises loyalty, devotion, friendship, justice and truth.

This star was awarded to 61 Australians in World War Two and 86 in the Vietnam War.

USA Flag

National Order
(Bao-Quoc Huan-Chuong)

Established in 1950
[Republic of Vietnam]

Ribbon colours

Red and yellow are the traditional auspicious colours of Vietnam. Red and yellow are also the National Flag colours of the Republic of Vietnam.

This order was awarded to 18 Australians in the Vietnam War.

Repubic of Vietnam Flag

Cross of Gallantry
(Anh-Dung Boi-Tinh/Croix de la Vallance)
Established in 1950
[Republic of Vietnam]

Cross of Gallantry
with Palm Unit Citation

Ribbon colours

Red and yellow are the traditional auspicious colours of Vietnam. Red and yellow are also the National Flag colours of the Republic of Vietnam.
The ribbon design was modeled on the French *Croix De Guerre* for overseas operations.

This cross was awarded to 340 Australians in the Vietnam War.

The *Cross of Gallantry with palm Unit Citation* was awarded to the Australian Army Training Team Vietnam (AATTV), the 8th Battalion Royal Australian Regiment (8RAR) and No.2 Squadron RAAF.

Repubic of Vietnam Flag

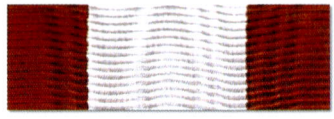

French Croix De Guerre
for overseas operations

Armed Forces Honour Medal
(Danh-Du Boi-Tinh)

Established in 1953
[Republic of Vietnam]

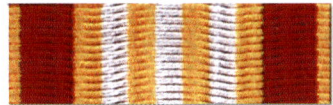

Ribbon colours

Red and yellow are the traditional auspicious colours of Vietnam. Red and yellow are also the National Flag colours of the Republic of Vietnam.

This medal was awarded to 51 Australians in the Vietnam War.

Repubic of Vietnam Flag

Zimbabwe Independence Medal
1980
[Zimbabwe]

Ribbon colours

Green, yellow red and black are the colours of the National Flag of Zimbabwe.

Zimbabwe Flag

Association and other Unofficial Medals worn by Australians

Many of the Association and other Unofficial Medals that are worn by Australians are not included in this publication, because their **ribbon colours have no known significance.**

Only those awards that appear in 'The Order of Wearing Australian Honours and Awards (dated 4 April 2002) or foreign awards for which official permission for wear has been obtained may be worn. Association and other unofficial commemorative medals are not authorised for wear and the wearing of such medals may constitute an offence under Section 83 of The Defence Act 1903.

Gallipoli Star
(unofficial medal)
[Australia]

Ribbon colours

Yellow represents the golden wattle flower of Australia.
Red represents the Armies.
Blue represents the Naval Forces.
Grey represents the silver fern of New Zealand.

This Star was approved by King George V for issue to the ANZACs. The idea was abandoned following objections from the British Parliament, as the Star was not for British troops at Gallipoli. Subsequently, it was privately manufactured in Australia and presented to the surviving Australian and New Zealand Gallipoli veterans in 1990, the 75th Anniversary of the Gallipoli landing.

Golden Wattle

New Zealand Silver Fern

Australian Logistic Support Forces Medal Vietnam

(unofficial medal)
[Australia]

Ribbon colours

Light blue represents the RAAF.
The wide red stripes represent the Australian Army.
Navy blue represents the RAN.
The narrow red stripes and yellow stripe represent the flag of the Republic of Vietnam.

Repubic of Vietnam Flag

Australian National Service Commemorative Medal 1951-1972

(National Servicemen's Association Medal)
[Australia]

Ribbon colours

Thin blue stripes represent the RAAF.
White stripes represent the RAN.
Red stripes represent the Australian Army.
Thick central royal blue and gold stripes are the livery colours on the Commonwealth of Australia Coat of Arms.

BCOF Regimental Medal

(BCOF Association Medal)
[Australia]

Ribbon colours

Green represents the Allied Armies.
Red represents the Allied Merchant Navies.
White represents the Allied Navies.
Blue represents the Allied Air Forces.

This medal was issued to members of the British Commonwealth Occupation Forces (BCOF), Japan, 1946-1952.

Citizen Military Forces and Reserve Forces Medal

(unofficial medal)
[Australia]

Ribbon colours

Navy blue, red and light blue represent the RAN, Australian Army and RAAF respectively.
White represents peacetime service.
Green represents homeland protection.

Conscripts Medal

(unofficial medal)
[Australia]

Ribbon colours

Red represents the Australian Army (70% of conscripts).
Navy blue represents the RAN (10% of conscripts).
Light blue represents the RAAF (20% of conscripts).

Emergency Services Medal

(unofficial medal)
[Australia]

Ribbon colours

Red represents the various fire brigades and fire services.
White represents the medical, nursing and ambulance services (including St John Ambulance).
Orange represents the emergency services, Salvation Army and Life Saving Services.
Navy blue represents police, corrective services, coast guard and security services.

Front Line Service Medal

(unofficial medal)
[Australia]

Ribbon colours

Yellow represents the deserts.
Red represents the Army, Infantry and the bloody sacrifices of the Infantry.
Green represents the jungle.

HMAS Sydney Vietnam Commemorative Medal 1965-1972

(unofficial medal)
[Australia]

Ribbon colours

Brown represents the colour of the muddy water at Vung Tau, South Vietnam.
Navy blue represents the RAN.
The two thick red stripes represent the Australian Army.
The three thin red stripes and four yellow stripes represent the flag of the Republic of Vietnam.
Members of the Australian Infantry Battalions (RAR) referred to HMAS Sydney as the 'Vung Tau Ferry' during the Vietnam War.

Repubic of Vietnam Flag

Military Remembrance Medal

(unofficial medal)
[Australia]

Ribbon colours

Purple represents remembrance.
Gold represents supreme sacrifice in defence of the Country.

Police Remembrance Medal

(unofficial medal)
[Australia]

Ribbon colours

Purple represents remembrance.
Gold represents supreme sacrifice in service to the public.
Black honours those killed in the line of duty.

Regular Forces Medal

(unofficial medal)
[Australia]

Ribbon colours

Navy blue, grey, red and light blue represent the RAN, Nursing Service, Australian Army and RAAF respectively.

Simpson Medal

(unofficial medal)
[Australia]

Ribbon colours

Red represents blood spilt in the service of the country. Purple represents remembrance.

Tobruk Siege Medal
(1941)
(Rats of Tobruk Association Medal)
[Australia]

Ribbon colours

Dark blue represents the Allied Navies.
Red represents the Allied Armies.
Light blue represents the Allied Air Forces.
Yellow represents the sands of the Western Desert.

2/4th Australian Infantry Battalion Medal
(2/4th Australian Infantry Battalion Association Medal)
[Australia]

2/4th Australian Infantry Battalion colour patch

Ribbon colours

Green and white are the colours of the 2/4th Australian Infantry Battalion colour patch (white over green - snow on the green pastures).

Pacific Islands Regiment Medal 1940-1990

[Papua New Guinea]

Ribbon colours

Red represents spilt blood.
Green represents the jungle.
Red and green are the colours of the Pacific Islands Regiment colour patch.

Medal recipients include members of the Papuan Infantry Battalion (PIB), which consisted of indigenous soldiers and some officers and senior non-commissioned officers of the Australian Imperial Force (AIF), during World War II.

Pacific Islands Regiment
Colour Patch

Active Service Cross of the Polish Forces in the West

(Krzyz Czynu Bojowego Polskich Sil Zbrojnych na Zachodzie)

1939-1945
(Unofficial Medal)
[Poland]

Ribbon colours

Red and white are the Polish national colours and national flag colours.

Azure (sky) blue and black are the colours of the **Order of Military Virtue**, which was established in 1792. Blue and black are the colours of the uniforms that were worn by Polish regiments in 1792. The significance of the green edge stripes is not known.

This cross was awarded to 600 to 800 surviving World War Two Australian *Rats of Tobruk* in the 1990s. This cross has never been offered to the Australian Government and is not authorised for wear.

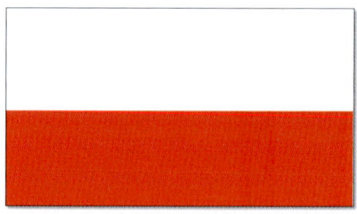

Polish Flag

Home Army Cross
(Krzyz Armii Krajowej [Krzyz AK])
1939-1945
(Unofficial Medal)
[Poland]

Ribbon colours

Red and white are the Polish national colours and national flag colours.
The six red stripes represent the six years of the existence of the *Home Army* (1939-1945).

This cross was awarded to a small number of RAAF crews who dropped supplies to the *Home Army* Partisans in German occupied Poland during World War Two. This cross has never been offered to the Australian Government and is not authorised for wear.

Polish Flag

Warsaw Uprising Cross
(Warszawski Krzyz Powstanczy)
1944
(Unofficial Medal)
[Poland]

Ribbon colours

Red and white are the Polish national colours and national flag colours.
Azure (sky) blue and black are the colours of the Order of Military Virtue, which was established in 1792.
Blue and black are the colours of the uniforms that were worn by Polish regiments in 1792.

This cross was awarded to a small number of RAAF crews who dropped supplies in Warsaw during the Uprising in 1944. This cross has never been offered to the Australian Government and is not authorised for wear.

Polish Flag

Medal Ribbon Manufacturing Process

The Wyedean Weaving Company Limited in England has been involved in the manufacture of medal ribbons for the majority of its 150 year existence. However, during World War Two, their factory in Coventry was completely destroyed in a bombing raid in 1942. The factory was quickly rebuilt and new machinery was built as the war effort was heavily dependent on their production of all types of military insignia.

Wyedean were pioneers in the narrow fabric industry and pioneered the manufacturing techniques of medal ribbons, refining them over the years. This is an ongoing process and even to this day, yarn compositions, manufacturing techniques and the looms on which these ribbons are woven are constantly being developed and improved.

The following is the ribbon manufacturing process in 2005:

Warp Yarns

In a standard full size 32mm wide medal ribbon, there are 252 threads across the warp (which are woven in lengthways down the ribbon and provide the visible colouring). The method of manufacturing medal ribbon uses fine quality, 2-fold nylon yarn, of around 110 Dtex (thickness), which is dyed to the appropriate colours under stringent control, to ensure solid colour throughout and a high degree of colour fastness. This is to eliminate fading over the forthcoming years and decades of possible display.

Weft Yarns

The weft yarns run across the width of the ribbon (in between the warp yarns) and bind or weave the warp yarns together. The weft is a similar yarn to that used in the warp and often white in colour or a colour which does not affect the appearance of the striping colours, nor appear noticeable where it becomes visible down the edge of the ribbons.

Warping

The warp yarns (on cones) are creeled up into a warping frame with appropriate number of ends (cones) according to the colour band widths. The warping up process is basically the reeling up of the required warp length onto a warp beam allowing 25% extra length to account for take up in the weaving process with colour stripings in the appropriate sequence.

Loom mounting

The warp ends on the beam are then threaded into the loom through back reeds, droppers and shafts, in the correct sequence and lastly slaved through a front reed (a type of metal comb) to hold them to the correct ribbon width. For a full size medal ribbon this process takes two people about four hours, as each of the 252 ends has to be individually knotted together by hand then passed to the second person who threads each warp end one by one through four separate yarn guiders in the loom.

Design

The majority of medal ribbons are plain multiple stripes, and are woven using one of the simplest weaving structures, known as plain weave. However, those ribbons with a more complex structure such as diagonal colours used in ribbons for the DFC, AFC, AFM or any non-linear pattern repeats become a jacquard weave construction. This requires significant design input with the creation of complex weave structures to create the required jacquard design.

Weaving

During the weaving process, all the warp and weft threads are carefully held under tension, using a variety of complex weighting devices, tension discs and tension springs within the loom. This enables the ribbon edges to be woven straight and even and the ribbon to have a smooth consistent appearance and lie flat when in a relaxed state.

The density of the weave is stringently controlled, so that the ribs are evenly spaced and consistent at 12 per cm, ensuring watermarking the correct patterning is achieved when required. The skills of the operator in setting the correct tensions and making continual adjustment during the weaving process take many years of experience to master.

Water Marking

After the weaving process, if required, the ribbon is water marked (usually only on one side of the ribbon, providing a face finish). This process is performed by passing the ribbon through a calendaring machine (a series of knurled and heated rollers), which applies the water marking or moire effect.

Blocking

The ribbon is then inspected, faults are mended or removed and the ribbon is reeled up, usually in 25 metre reels, and stored for sale against requirements as they arise.

Stocks

Wyedean tend to stock a range of ribbons representing those with living history, which is where there is regular volume demand by the holders and wearers of medals. Other ribbons are made to order, usually requiring a higher pricing structure in view of the smaller quantities required.

Silk or nylon?

During World War Two, Wyedean was heavily involved in medal ribbon production. In those days pure silk was used to weave the ribbon. However, during the war this became difficult to obtain, as most of the silk was channelled into the manufacture of parachutes.

About this time, a new product became available called nylon. The then directors of Wyedean developed ribbons in this new material, and proposed to the War Office that it be used as an alternative to silk ribbons. The War Office agreed, and the proposal went through higher authorities for approval. The proposal came to the notice of King George VI. He immediately declared that "such honours are awarded for acts of bravery and devotion to duty and as such, only the highest qualities of material should be used". He promptly overruled this decision and personally arranged for silk to be diverted away from parachute production to Wyedean, so that the medal ribbons could continue to be manufactured in pure silk.

Since then, principles of economy have overridden this noble standpoint, and nylon eventually superseded the use of pure silk at the behest of those holding the purse strings. Medal ribbons are still, on rare occasions, woven in pure silk, but because it is no longer universally utilised, the costs of production and silk processing are astronomic in comparison with nylon.

The Order of Wearing Australian Honours and Awards

The Governor-General directs that the positioning of the following awards, within the order of precedence in which Australian Orders, Decorations and Medals should be worn, be notified for general information:

- Ambulance Service Medal,
- Emergency Services Medal,
- Australian Active Service Medal 1945-1975,
- International Force East Timor Medal,
- Humanitarian Overseas Service Medal,
- 80th Anniversary Armistice Remembrance Medal,
- Australian Sports Medal,
- Centenary Medal, Defence Long Service Medal,
- Australian Cadet Forces Service Medal,
- Anniversary of National Service 1951-1972 Medal,
- Australian Defence Medal.

The Schedule, together with the Annexes to the Schedule, incorporates the new positioning of these awards and supersedes that notified in Commonwealth of Australia Gazette No.S208 of 17 June 1996.

Honours and Awards listed in the Schedule and Annexes in **BOLD** print are:

- those within the Australian System of Honours and Awards;
- those conferred by The Sovereign in exercise of the Royal Prerogative;
- those within the Order of St John; and
- foreign awards, the acceptance and wearing of which have been authorised by the Governor-General.

The Schedule

VICTORIA CROSS (1)	**VC**
George Cross	GC
CROSS OF VALOUR	**CV**
KNIGHT/LADY OF THE GARTER	**KG/LG**
KNIGHT/LADY OF THE THISTLE	**KT/LT**
Knight/Dame Grand Cross of the Order of the Bath	GCB
ORDER OF MERIT	**OM**
KNIGHT/DAME OF THE ORDER OF AUSTRALIA (2)	**AK/AD**
Knight/Dame Grand Cross of the Order of St Michael and St George	GCMG
KNIGHT/DAME GRAND CROSS OF THE ROYAL VICTORIAN ORDER	**GCVO**
Knight/Dame Grand Cross of the Order of the British Empire	GBE
COMPANION OF THE ORDER OF AUSTRALIA	**AC**
Companion of Honour	CH
Knight/Dame Commander of the Order of the Bath	KCB/CB
Knight/Dame Commander of the Order of St Michael and St George	KCMG/CMG
KNIGHT/DAME COMMANDER OF THE ROYAL VICTORIAN ORDER	**KCVO/DCVO**
Knight/Dame Commander of the Order of the British Empire	KBE/DBE
Knight Bachelor (NB: Confers title of "Sir" - no postnominals)	
OFFICER OF THE ORDER OF AUSTRALIA`	**AO**
Companion of the Order of the Bath	CB
Companion of the Order of St Michael and St George	CMG
COMMANDER OF THE ROYAL VICTORIAN ORDER	CVO
Commander of the Order of the British Empire	CBE
STAR OF GALLANTRY	**SG**
STAR OF COURAGE	**SC**
Companion of the Distinguished Service Order	DSO
DISTINGUISHED SERVICE CROSS	**DSC**
MEMBER OF THE ORDER OF AUSTRALIA	**AM**
LIEUTENANT OF THE ROYAL VICTORIAN ORDER	**LVO**
Officer of the Order of the British Empire	OBE
Companion of the Imperial Service Order	ISO
MEMBER OF THE ROYAL VICTORIAN ORDER	**MVO**
Member of the Order of the British Empire	MBE
CONSPICUOUS SERVICE CROSS	**CSC**
NURSING SERVICE CROSS	**NSC**
Royal Red Cross (1st Class)	RRC
Distinguished Service Cross	DSC
Military Cross	MC
Distinguished Flying Cross	DFC
Air Force Cross	AFC
Royal Red Cross (2nd Class)	ARRC

MEDAL FOR GALLANTRY	MG
BRAVERY MEDAL	BM
DISTINGUISHED SERVICE MEDAL	DSM
PUBLIC SERVICE MEDAL	PSM
AUSTRALIAN POLICE MEDAL	APM
AUSTRALIAN FIRE SERVICE MEDAL	AFSM
AMBULANCE SERVICE MEDAL	ASM
EMERGENCY SERVICES MEDAL	ESM
MEDAL OF THE ORDER OF AUSTRALIA	OAM
ORDER OF ST JOHN (3)	
Distinguished Conduct Medal	DCM
Conspicuous Gallantry Medal	CGM
George Medal	GM
CONSPICUOUS SERVICE MEDAL	**CSM**
AUSTRALIAN ANTARCTIC MEDAL (4)	**AAM**
Queen's Police Medal for Gallantry	QPM
Queen's Fire Service Medal for Gallantry	QFSM
Distinguished Service Medal	DSM
Military Medal	MM
Distinguished Flying Medal	DFM
Air Force Medal	AFM
Queen's Gallantry Medal	QGM
ROYAL VICTORIAN MEDAL	**RVM**
British Empire Medal	BEM
Queen's Police Medal for Distinguished Service	QPM
Queen's Fire Service Medal for Distinguished Service	QFSM
COMMENDATION FOR GALLANTRY	
COMMENDATION FOR BRAVE CONDUCT	
Queen's Commendation for Brave Conduct	
COMMENDATION FOR DISTINGUISHED SERVICE	
War medals, campaign medals, active service medals and service medals, (see Annex 1)	
POLICE OVERSEAS SERVICE MEDAL (5)	
HUMANITARIAN OVERSEAS SERVICE MEDAL (5)	
CIVILIAN SERVICE MEDAL 1939-1945	
Polar Medal	
Imperial Service Medal	
Coronation, Jubilee, Remembrance and Commemorative medals, (in order of date of receipt) (see Annex 2)	
DEFENCE FORCE SERVICE MEDAL	
RESERVE FORCE DECORATION	RFD
RESERVE FORCE MEDAL	
DEFENCE LONG SERVICE MEDAL	
NATIONAL MEDAL	
AUSTRALIAN DEFENCE MEDAL	
AUSTRALIAN CADET FORCES SERVICE MEDAL	
CHAMPION SHOTS MEDAL	
Long Service Medals (6)	
ANNIVERSARY OF NATIONAL SERVICE 1951-1972 MEDAL	
Independence and Anniversary Medals, (in order of date of receipt)	
Foreign Awards, (in order of date of authorisation of their acceptance and wearing)	

Notes:

1. Refers to the Imperial Victoria Cross and the Victoria Cross for Australia.

2. Provision for further awards at this level within the Order of Australia was removed by Her Majesty The Queen on 3 March 1986 on the advice of the Prime Minister.

3. Listed to indicate where any awards within the Order of St John should be worn.

4. The Australian Antarctic Medal was known as the Antarctic Medal until 18 December 1997.

5. Clasps to these medals should be worn on the ribbon in order of date of receipt.

6. Refers to Imperial efficiency and long service awards.

General Note:

The Unit Citation for Gallantry, the Meritorious Unit Citation and the Group Bravery Citation are not positioned in The Order of Wearing Australian Honours and Awards. For members of uniformed services, they should be worn in accordance with the dress rules of the particular Service concerned. Civilian personnel awarded the Group Bravery Citation should wear the insignia on the left lapel or left breast. Should other honours or awards have been awarded, the Group Bravery Citation should be worn centrally, approx 10mm above these.

Annex 1
to Schedule on the Order of Wearing
Australian Honours and Awards

WAR MEDALS, CAMPAIGN MEDALS, ACTIVE SERVICE MEDALS AND SERVICE MEDALS (1901 onwards)

South African War

Queen's South Africa Medal
King's South Africa Medal

World War I

1914 Star
1914-15 Star (1*)
British War Medal
Mercantile Marine War Medal
Victory Medal
Naval General Service Medal 1915-62 (2* & 3*)
General Service Medal 1918-62 (2* & 3*)

World War II

1939-45 Star
Atlantic Star (4*)
Air Crew Europe Star (4*)
Africa Star
Pacific Star (5*)
Burma Star (5*)
Italy Star
France and Germany Star (4*)
Defence Medal
War Medal, 1939-45
AUSTRALIA SERVICE MEDAL 1939-45

Post-World War II

AUSTRALIAN ACTIVE SERVICE MEDAL 1945-1975 (3*)
Korea Medal
United Nations Service Medal for Korea (6*)
Naval General Service Medal 1915-62 (2* & 3*)
General Service Medal 1918-62 (2* & 3*)
General Service Medal 1962 (3*)

VIETNAM MEDAL
VIETNAM LOGISTIC AND SUPPORT MEDAL (7*)
AUSTRALIAN ACTIVE SERVICE MEDAL (3*)
INTERNATIONAL FORCE EAST TIMOR MEDAL
AUSTRALIAN SERVICE MEDAL 1945-1975 (3*)
AUSTRALIAN SERVICE MEDAL (3*)
RHODESIA MEDAL

Notes:

1*. Recipients of the 1914 Star are not eligible for the award of the 1914-15 Star.

2*. The order of wearing of the Naval General Service Medal 1915-62 and General Service Medal 1918-62 (Army and Air Force) will vary from person to person depending on when the person earned the first clasp. If the first clasp relates to service between World War I and World War II, the medals should be worn immediately after World War I war medals. If the first clasp relates to service after 2 September 1945, the medals should be worn immediately after the United Nations Service Medal for Korea.

3*. Clasps to these medals should be worn on the ribbon in order of date of receipt.

4*. Only one of these three Stars could be awarded to an individual. Should a person have qualified for two of these awards, the Star first earned is worn with the Clasp of the second Star. Only one Star and one Clasp may be worn even if the person qualified for all three Stars.

5*. Only one of these two Stars could be awarded to an individual. Should a person have qualified for both the Pacific Star and the Burma Star, the Star first earned was awarded together with the appropriate Clasp denoting the service that would have qualified for the other Star.

6*. Uniquely, although a foreign award, the United Nations Service Medal for Korea is worn immediately after the Korea Medal. All other foreign awards for which official permission has been given to accept and wear are worn as Foreign Awards.

7*. A person who has been awarded the Vietnam Medal, or who is eligible for the award of the Vietnam Medal, is not eligible for the award of the Vietnam Logistic and Support Medal.

Annex 2
to Schedule on the Order of Wearing
Australian Honours and Awards

CORONATION MEDALS, JUBILEE MEDALS, REMEMBRANCE MEDALS AND COMMEMORATIVE MEDALS (1901 onwards)

KING EDWARD VII CORONATION MEDAL
KING GEORGE V CORONATION MEDAL
KING GEORGE V SILVER JUBILEE MEDAL
KING GEORGE VI CORONATION MEDAL
QUEEN ELIZABETH II CORONATION MEDAL
QUEEN ELIZABETH II SILVER JUBILEE MEDAL
80th ANNIVERSARY ARMISTICE REMEMBRANCE MEDAL
AUSTRALIAN SPORTS MEDAL
CENTENARY MEDAL

Bibliography

ABBOTT, P.E. & TAMPLIN J.M.A.
British Gallantry Awards.
London, Nimrod Dix & Co., 1981.

CARTER, Thomas and LONG, William Henry.
War Medals of the British Army and how they were won.
London, Norie and Wilson, 1893.

FOX-DAVIES, Arthur Charles.
The Book of Public Arms.
London, T. C. & E. C. Jack, 1915.

GLYDE, Keith.
Distinguishing Colour Patches of the Australian Military Forces 1915-1951 - A Reference Guide.
Claremont, Tasmania, K. Glyde, 1999.

GORDON, Major L.L.
British Battles and Medals (Fifth Edition).
London, Spink & Son Ltd, 1979.

GREBERT, Rick.
Australian Victoria Cross Recipients.
Sydney, [unpublished], 1990.

GREBERT, Rick.
Fragments of Australian Military History.
Sydney, NSW Military Historical Society, 1988.

GREBERT, Rick.
New South Wales Sudan Contingent 1885 Some Biographical and Personal Details [with statistics].
Sydney, NSW Military Historical Society Inc., 1998.

JOCELYN, Capt. Arthur.
Awards of Honour.
Adam & Charles Black, 1956.

KIRKLAND, Frederick (Ed.).
Sometimes Forgotten.
Sydney, Plaza Historical Service, 1990.

LITHERLAND A.R. & SIMPKIN B.T.
Spinks Standard Catalogue of British and Associated Orders, Decorations and Medals with Valuations.
London, Spink & Son Limited, 1990.

MACOBOY, Sterling.
What Flower is that?
Sydney, Weldon Publishing, 1991.

MATON, Michael.
Imperial Orders to Australians 1901-1989.
Sydney, Michael Maton, 1999.

MATON, Michael.
The National Honours and Awards of Australia.
Kenthurst, Kangaroo Press Ltd., 1995.

MATON, Michael.
The Order of the British Empire to Australians 1917-1989.
Sydney, Michael Maton, 1998.

McNEILL, Ian.
The Team, Australian Army Advisers in Vietnam 1962-1972.
St Lucia, Qld., University of Queensland Press, 1984.

McDOWELL, Charles P.
Military and Naval Decorations of the United States.
Virginia, Quest Publishing Company, 1984.

MERICKA, Vaclav.
The Book of Orders and Decorations.
London, Hamlyn, 1975.

PAMM, Anthony N.
Honours and Rewards in the British Empire and Commonwealth.
Vermont, 1995.

PATERSON, David.
Collecting Military Medals and Decorations.
London, Stanley Gibbons Publications Ltd., 1979.

SYLVESTER, John Jr. and FOSTER, Frank C. Jr.
The Decorations and Medals of the Republic of Vietnam and Her Allies 1950-1975.
Fountain Inn, South Carolina, Medals of America, 1995.

TANCRED, George,
Historical Record of Medals and Honorary Distinctions.
London, Spink & Son, 1891.

TAPRELL DORLING, Captain H.,
Ribbons and Medals.
London, George Philip & Son Limited, 1974.

WILLIAMS, R. D.
Medals to Australia with Valuations.
Melbourne, Downie's, 2000.

- **Campaign and Operational Medals Awarded to the Australian Defence Force.**
Canberra, Department of Defence, 1999.

- **Chambers Dictionary of Etymology (20 Volumes).**
Edinburgh, Harrap Publishers Ltd., 2000.

- **The Oxford English Dictionary (Second Edition) [20 Volumes].**
Oxford, Oxford University Press, 1989.

- **The Order of Precedence for Wearing of US Decorations and Service Medals**
(AR 600-8-22).

- **The Order of Wearing Australian Honours and Awards**
Government House, Canberra, 4 April 2002.

Index

A

Acacia Pycnantha, 44
Active Service Cross of the Polish Forces in the West, 114
Afghanistan Campaign Medal, 57
Africa Star, 34
Air Crew Europe Star, 34
Allied Victory Medal, 15, 32
Ambulance Service Medal, 50
Anniversary of National Service 1951-1972 Medal, 69
Armed Forces Honour Medal (Vietnam), 101
Association Medals, 103
Atlantic Star, 33
Australian Active Service Medal (1945-75), 24, 54
Australian Active Service Medal (since 1975), 56
Australian Antarctic Medal, 52
Australian Army Training Team Vietnam, 100
Australian Cadet Forces Service Medal, 68
Australian Defence Medal, 67
Australian Fire Service Medal, 50
Australian Honours System, 5, 44
Australian Logistic Support Forces Medal Vietnam (unofficial), 105
Australian National Service Commemorative Medal (unofficial), 106
Australian Police Medal, 49
Australian Service Medal 1939-45, 38
Australian Service Medal (1945-75), 24, 58
Australian Service Medal (since 1975), 58
Australian Sports Medal, 63

B

BCOF Regimental Medal (Association Medal), 106
Blocking, 119
Boer War (see South Africa)
Boxer Rebellion (see Third China War Medal 1900)
Bravery Medal, 48

British Empire Medal, 22
British Orders, Decorations and Medals, 5, 13
Bronze Cross (Netherlands), 89
Bronze Star (USA), 98
Burma Star, 35

C

Centenary Medal, 63
Champion Shots Medal, 68
China War Medal (see Third China War Medal)
Citizen Military Forces and Reserve Forces Medal (unofficial), 107
Civilian Service Medal 1939-1945, 61
Commander of the Order of the British Empire, 22
Commendation for Brave Conduct, 53
Commendation for Distinguished Service, 53
Commendation for Gallantry, 52
Companion of the Order of Australia, 44
Conscripts Medal (unofficial), 107
Conspicuous Service Cross, 46
Conspicuous Service Medal, 51
Croix De Guerre (France), 100
Cross of Gallantry (Vietnam), 100
Cross of Gallantry Unit Citation (Vietnam), 100
Cross of Merit (Netherlands), 90
Cross of Valour (Australia), 43
Cross of Valour (Poland), 93

D

Dame Commander of the Order of the British Empire, 22
Dame Grand Cross of the Order of the British Empire, 22
Dame of the Order of Australia, 44
Defence Force Service Medal, 24, 64
Defence Long Service Medal, 65
Defence Medal, 37
Distinguished Conduct Medal, 23-24
Distinguished Flying Cross (USA), 96
Distinguished Service Cross, 46
Distinguished Service Cross (USA), 95
Distinguished Service Medal, 48

Distinguished Service Medal (USA), 95
Distinguished Service Order, 11, 23

E

East Timor (see International Force East Timor)
Egypt Medal, 27
Emergency Services Medal, 51
Emergency Services Medal (unofficial), 108

F

Flanders Poppy, 62, 67
Flying Cross (Netherlands), 90
Foreign Orders, Decorations and Medals, 5, 13, 87
France and Germany Star, 36
Front Line Service Medal (unofficial), 108

G

Gallipoli Star, 104
George Cross, 18
Golden Wattle, 44, 46, 51, 104

H

HMAS Sydney Vietnam Commemorative Medal (unofficial), 109
Home Army Cross (Poland), 115
Humanitarian Overseas Service Medal, 60

I

International Force East Timor Medal, 56
Iraq Campaign Medal, 57
Italy Star, 36

J

Jacquard Weave, 118

K

Khedive's Star, 27
King's South Africa Medal (see South Africa)
Knight Commander of the Order of the British Empire, 22
Knight Grand Cross of the Order of the British Empire, 22
Knight of the Order of Australia, 44
Korea Medal, 24, 39

L

Liberation of Kuwait Medal (Kuwait), 88
Liberation of Kuwait Medal (Saudi Arabia), 94
Loom Mounting, 118

M

Maori War Medal (see New Zealand Medal)
Medal for Acts of Humanity, 91
Medal for Gallantry, 49
Medal of the Order of Australia, 44
Medal Ribbon manufacturing process, 117
Member of the Order of Australia, 44
Member of the Order of the British Empire, 22
Mercantile Marine War Medal, 31
Meritorious Unit Citation, 70
Military Remembrance Medal (unofficial), 110
Military Riband of England, 11, 14, 21, 23, 25-26, 42
Mimosa, 44
Miniature Medals, 12
Mons Star (see 1914 Star)

N

Natal Rebellion Medal 1906, 29
National Medal, 24, 66
National Order (Vietnam), 99
National Service Medal (see Anniversary of National Service Medal)
NATO Former Yugoslavia Medal, 86
NATO Kosovo Medal, 86
Naval Riband of England, 11, 14, 42

New Zealand Medal 1845-1866, 26
Nile River, 27
Nursing Service Cross, 47
Nylon, 117, 119-120

O

Officer of the Order of Australia, 44
Officer of the Order of the British Empire, 22
Order of Australia, 44
Order of Merit, 21
Order of Military Virtue (Poland), 93, 114, 116
Order of Orange Nassau (Netherlands), 89
Order of St Michael and St George, 21
Order of the Bath, 20-21
Order of the British Empire, 22
Order of the Garter, 10, 18-19, 21
Order of the Thistle, 20
Order of wearing Australian Honours and Awards, 5, 121

P

Pacific Islands Regiment Medal (unofficial), 113
Pacific Star, 35
Papua New Guinea Independence Medal, 92
Papua New Guinea 10th Anniversary of Independence Medal, 92
Parachutes, 119-120
Police Overseas Service Medal, 60
Police Remembrance Medal (unofficial), 110
Public Service Medal, 49

Q

Queen's South Africa Medal (see South Africa)

R

Rainbow, 32
Regular Forces Medal (unofficial), 111
Republic of Vietnam Campaign Medal (Star), 24, 40
Reserve Force Decoration, 64

Reserve Force Medal, 65
Rhodesia Medal, 59
Ribbon Bars, 12

S

Silk, 119
Silver Star (USA), 96
Simpson Medal (unofficial), 111
Soldiers Medal (USA), 97
Soudan (Sudan) War, 27
South Africa, 15, 28-29
South Vietnam Campaign Medal (see Republic of Vietnam Campaign Medal)
Special Air Service Regiment, 70
Star of Courage, 45
Star of Gallantry, 45

T

Third China War Medal, 28
Tobruk Siege Medal (Association Medal), 112, 114

U

Unit Citation for Gallantry, 70
United Nations Medals, 5, 71
    UN Advance Mission in Cambodia, 80
    UN Assistance for Rwanda, 84
    UN Assistance Mission in East Timor / UN Transitional Administration in East Timor, 85
    UN Disengagement Observer Force - Golan Heights, 76
    UN Emergency Force II, 75
    UN Headquarters, 72
    UN Iran / Iraq Military Observers Group, 77
    UN Military Observer Force in India and Pakistan, 73
    UN Mission for the Referendum in Western Sahara, 79
    UN Operations in Mozambique, 82
    UN Operations in Somalia, 82
    UN Operations in the Congo, 74
    UN Peacekeeping Force in Cyprus, 75
    UN Protection Force, 81
    UN Service Medal Korea, 24, 39, 73

UN Special Service Medal, 79
UN Transition Assistance Group, 78
UN Transitional Authority in Cambodia, 81
UN Truce Supervision Organisation, 72
UN Verification Mission in Guatemala, 83
UN Yemen Observer mission, 74
Unofficial Medals, 5, 103

V

Victoria Cross, 14-17, 42
Victoria Cross for Australia, 42
Victory Medal (see Allied Victory Medal)
Vietnam Logistic and Support Medal, 55
Vietnam Medal, 24, 40

W

Waikato Regiments, 26
War Medal 1939-45 (Great Britain), 37
Warp Yarns, 117
Warping, 118
Warsaw Uprising Cross (Poland), 116
Water Marking, 119
Waterloo Medal, 11, 25
Wattle (see Golden Wattle)
Weaving, 118
Weft Yarns, 117
Wyedean Weaving Co Ltd, 6, 117, 119-120

XYZ

Zimbabwe Independence Medal, 59, 102
Zulu Rising (see Natal Rebellion Medal)

1914 Star, 30, 32
1914-15 Star, 15, 30, 32
1939-45 Star, 33
80th Anniversary Armistice Remembrance Medal, 62
2/4th Australian Infantry Battalion Medal (Association Medal), 112